KINGDOM
CONFIDENCE

**DEMONSTRATING THE *POWER, AUTHORITY,*
AND *INFLUENCE* OF GOD IN YOUR
LIFE & BUSINESS**

All Scriptures are taken from the NIV unless otherwise noted.

ISBN 13: 979-8-5830460-0-3

Printed in the United States of America

Contact Info:
Jesse A. Cole, Jr.
Kingdom Mogul Coaching
P.O. Box 442
Hazel Park, MI 48030
(810) 354-5464
www.CoachJesseCole.com

DEDICATION

This book is dedicated to those who believe there is no separation between their spiritual life and their business. My hope is that you continue to share your message and use your God-given talents to show up in the marketplace with authenticity and boldness.

TABLE OF CONTENTS

INTRODUCTION

For a long time, I struggled with being confident in who I was. I knew that I had gifts and talents to offer the world. I knew that I could add value to any environment I was a part of, but there were some issues that I had to overcome. Some of the issues were planted inside of me when I was a kid. Others I planted myself through unhealthy decisions I made. Both were gradually eating away at my confidence and deteriorating my potential.

But God began to show me how to overcome those issues. For about 24 months, He began to expose and heal the places I had neglected or never knew were there. Through that process, He showed me what it looked like to be authentic and transparent. I began to be ok with being flawed in some areas, and I learned how to double down in the areas where I was strong. And He used both to bring me to a place of active obedience through graceful accountability.

Throughout the process, I would write down what I learned and any revelation that I had discovered. Over time, I began to see a difference in how I thought and carried myself. People began to give me unsolicited feedback on the difference they were seeing. I kept hearing the words "relatable" and "authentic". To me, it just felt like growth, an unforced evolution that felt natural and refreshing.

Before the transition, most of my branding pictures consisted of a suit and tie. I wanted to project a polished image. That's what I saw all of the other speakers doing, so I thought I had to be seen that way for me to be respected in the marketplace. Don't get me wrong, I still like to dress up, but I slowly began to see a change in how I showed up. One of my mentors asked about the minor changes I had made in my marketing approach, and the only example I could give is that I just took my tie off. It was like God was showing me that He needed me to be a relatable authority in the space He called me to occupy.

I figured that I wasn't the only one who felt a blockage in their impact and effectiveness. I believed that more people were just as gifted and anointed as I was. Still, something was stopping them from demonstrating their purpose and assignment with boldness. So I prayed about a way to encourage and equip them using the process that God took me through. God responded immediately in an unlikely way.

On August 17, 2020, Holy Spirit prompted me to post a video on my social media pages inviting people to register for a coaching program. He told me to call it Kingdom Confidence. He said that I would provide one hour of virtual coaching every Monday at 7 pm for six weeks at no cost to the registrants. Here's the interesting part, I didn't even have a coaching program framework for this; all I had were notes that I had scribbled on a white poster board. And even though I had private coaching clients, I had never done an online group coaching program before. All of this was new to me. I didn't have a marketing campaign, nor did I do any market research to see if this was even a viable solution. So with a rough draft of thoughts and minimal instruction from Holy Spirit, I posted that video with the audacity to believe that at least one person would see the value in this opportunity.

I felt like this was a setup, a pivotal moment in my life where God wanted to open up the windows of heaven and test my faith. I was up for the challenge, so I had no choice but to be obedient. I set a goal to register 40 people for this beta program. So, for the next few weeks, I marketed and promoted with the direction of Holy Spirit. If He told me to post a video or some content to promote the program, I did. If I didn't hear His instruction, I didn't move. It was that simple for me; a spirit-led marketing and promotion campaign for sure. Unconventional, but it worked for me.

Over the next few weeks, the registrations trickled through. By the end of the registration period, 35 people had signed up, and an average of 22 people from all over the United States and internationally showed up every week for the coaching calls. I was clear that my assignment was to create an environment where Holy Spirit could do what He needed to do in the lives of God's people. I was just the facilitator of the environment, and the students showed up and did the work. During the coaching process, marriages were restored, businesses were launched, dreams were re-ignited, hearts were humbled and healed. Some people learned how to rest in God, while others learned how to show up in the marketplace with force. The transformation that took place can only be attributed to God. I can't take credit for that. I won't take credit for that. This book was birthed out of that experience.

Kingdom Confidence is a movement of obedience. One has to be willing to believe what the Word says about them and submit to Holy Spirit's unconventional leading in their lives. God is a rule breaker. He desires to break the rule of the world over our lives. I'm excited to share the Kingdom Confidence concept with people like you. Individuals who are talented but maybe you don't feel worthy enough to do the work. You have dreams and aspirations. You can see the next level of your success, but something is stopping you from taking that next step. Maybe you are in a place that no longer supports the person you desire to be, and there is an internal conflict raging between your limiting beliefs and the radical pull of your faith. This book is for those who need the structure and accountability to lead unapologetically in their specific area of impact. The purpose of this framework is to help you transform your mindset and heart concerning your purpose and assignment, boldly walk in your abilities and capabilities, and affirm your value.

I believe God will teach you how to identify and overcome your limiting beliefs and embrace His confidence in your life and business. This is a call to contentment; a vehicle for teaching you how to yield to God and trust Him to lead you into an encounter of transformation to receive His best for you. You have a Kingdom message that is designed to break yokes and help change lives. Your obedience and consistency can have an eternal impact on those you are called to serve. If you want to understand your calling and how you can best serve God's people with your life & business, you need Kingdom Confidence. I hope that as you read this book, you will write down what Holy Spirit is revealing to you and be obedient to what you hear because 99% of obedience is equal to 100% disobedience.

Let's Work!

KINGDOM
CONFIDENCE

DEMONSTRATING THE *POWER, AUTHORITY,*
AND *INFLUENCE* OF GOD IN YOUR
LIFE & BUSINESS

Chapter 1

The Sound of Your Assignment

*"Before I formed you in the womb I knew you, before you
were born I set you apart; I appointed you
as a prophet to the nations."*

Jeremiah 1:5

Sound has been used throughout history as a tool of
action; it is a signifier. Whether it's the whistle of a train, the
bark of a dog, or the steady rhythm of a bass drum, sound
contains the data that gives us a clue for how we should
respond. Your assignment has a sound too. It pierces through
the barriers of time and distance. It connects with the hearts
of men and women whose souls have been longing for a
solution and revelation that can lead to their transformation.
It is a sound that only the people that need what you have
can appreciate.

It's a resonating sound. An identifier, if you will. Every
time you demonstrate your assignment, it's as if you're
ringing an alarm—a call to action. Your assignment leads
people to a spiritual truth in a practical way. It's the pathway

to their destiny, and it helps them discover Christ for themselves.

To some of you, this may be exciting news. You've been waiting for the extra push to begin walking in your kingdom authority. For others, this word of knowledge can be a little scary. There may be some lingering hesitation that you're holding on to. Let me speak to the little bit of doubt that might be present as you read this. You are valuable, and you have been called and chosen to live a purposeful and significant life. I know you've probably heard that before, but it's true. It's not just an inspirational anecdote; this mindset is important because it will strengthen your confidence to show up how God needs you to show up. This chapter is filled with cultivating questions to help you break up the fallow ground of doubt or unfruitful contention.

But I'm sure you have questions, right? Questions like: Who called me? What am I called to do? Who am I called to, and what are they missing? Why am I called to them, and why is my gifting a part of their solution? I'll address those questions throughout this book in a non-linear way. The answers will be interwoven between stories and kingdom principles, and my prayer is that you will hear God for yourself and be obedient about taking action. In most cases, you won't have to create anything new; you'll just be refining what you already have to meet the needs of the people you're called and assigned to.

How Do You Know When You've Been Called?

This principle plays out well in the life of Moses. Here you have a man who was born into what could be considered a lower-class family. A man saved from being slaughtered at birth, rescued by pharaoh's daughter, raised in a highly visible position in the royal palace, and then because of extenuating circumstances, finds himself living a secluded, humble life. Then one day, God decides to interrupt his modest routine and flip his life upside down. This is what I call a Burning Bush moment. A Holy Interruption, if you will. It disrupts your regular routing. Often you're the only one who can hear God speaking to you. It's an internal shaking that can cause you to reevaluate your entire existence. It is God's way of breaking the flow of mediocrity and introducing you to a life of significance.

Reinvention Strategist, Marshawn Evans-Daniels, said, "Disruption is an invitation to enter a higher dimension of destiny." You are awakened to a cause or kingdom assignment that only you can do, but you've run away from it because the task just seemed too big for you to even consider. Perhaps you haven't known about it, and this shaking helps you sift through the distractions to see that cause more clearly. Whatever being the case, you've been called to something higher than what you've lent your time and energy to. God is speaking to you right now to check your heart. What do I mean?

When you check your heart, you willingly decrease your carnal expectations of success and open up to God's plan for your life. You take into consideration what could happen if you were obedient. This takes faith because we work so hard to build our ideal lives, brands, businesses, families, etc., but how often do we ask God, "Father, is this *Your* best for me?"

We can become so consumed with stocking our trophy cases with awards and medals that become a testament to our "hard work," but these trophies will soon perish. So what are we doing it all for anyway? Matthew 6:21 says plainly, "Your heart will always be where your treasure is (CEV)." So when we check *our* hearts, it gives God a chance to pour out *His* heart into us. This requires a bold attempt to relinquish your schedule to serve God's plan and then convert that initial attempt into a lifestyle of submission.

Just like Moses had his Burning Bush moment, you will have yours as well. And I can tell you from experience; you may have multiple occurrences where God will call you higher and into an uncomfortable realm to do a greater work where you'll have to depend on Him. My friend, there is a cause that you've been called to, and it fits perfectly with your life experiences. You've lived the curriculum to provide a solution to someone's problem, answer a question that hasn't been asked yet, and to be the conduit of a breakthrough for some thirsty soul.

Your Experiences Will Prepare You For The Calling

As it pertains to actualizing our calling, often, we forfeit the power of God by replacing it with the power of our fear. Meaning, God wants to use our life, the good and the perceived bad, to get His message into the hands of those who need it and you. But our genius get's in the way. Sometimes we can be so intellectual that we can't be truly effective. In most cases, being intellect-led can minimize God's impact. Now, hear my heart and let me be clear; common sense is a tool. Your education is a tool. Critical thinking is a tool. But sometimes, overuse or inappropriate use of these tools can get in the way of God using you how He needs to.

Subsequently, we can overthink it when God only needs us to get out of the way. In the introduction of this book, I shared how I launched the Kingdom Confidence Academy. It was raw and, by industry standards, not well planned out. But imagine if I decided to analyze the market and strategize the perfect launch campaign. I'd probably still be trying to make the marketing look just right, and I would've missed out on what God was trying to do at the moment. That simple act of obedience led to results that I could've never predicted or planned for.

This lesson taught me that if we desire to be truly effective in the kingdom, we must learn how to be obedient to whatever the moment requires. I already had everything I needed to lead that group. I had a combination of the word of God, real-life stories, and a testimony of transformation to share. I didn't have to find any new content or manufacture an experience to impress them. I just had to be transparent and humble, and He did the rest. God knew that was all I needed, it was more than enough to serve that particular community, and He trusted me to creatively put it all together like only I could.

Coaching is a big part of my assignment. I love it because I get to learn about people on a deeper level, which helps me to serve them better. People have shared their stories of domestic violence, losing a child, being bullied, marital issues, drug addiction, sexual abuse, and many other life experiences. But here's the interesting part, they aren't the only ones who have ever experienced those things, but their story is unique to them, and there is someone who will be able to relate to their trial and will be encouraged by their breakthrough. I get to show them how their transformation has equipped them to serve a diverse group of people who need what they have. The same applies to you.

There is a connection between what you've lived through and who can learn from you. So in terms of being prepared for your calling, God will expose your life alignment. Your life alignment is how your experiences, trauma, and triumphs merge with the message He needs you to share.

Here are a few experimental exercises that can help you identify what that could look like for you. Feel free to write the answers to these questions on a separate sheet of paper:

Describe an experience where you felt completely vulnerable. What happened, how did you respond, and what lessons did you learn from that experience?

Describe a time where you felt completely fulfilled. What were you doing? Describe the emotions that you felt.

Imagine that you are at the end of your life, and you have an opportunity to share a special message with those you love. What would you say? Why do you think that message is important?

Your answers to these questions will spark a flame of discovery that can illuminate your purpose and assignment. Your purpose is *why* you were created. Your assignment is *how* you demonstrate it in your everyday life. You don't have to look outside of you for the answers because the answers exist inside of you.

When you survey the Bible, God used people who had unique experiences to get His message out into the world. The evidence of their struggle is what made them relatable to those they were assigned to. People were more apt to listen to the messenger because they could see a piece of themselves inside the messenger. Your storied background is the key to unlock someone else's breakthrough. And when you share it boldly and unapologetically, as you willingly disseminate your truth, it will hit its intended target.

What Is Your Burden?

Everybody has a burden or cause that they are assigned to. None of us are detached from the pull of humanity. We all have a specific kingdom assignment to complete. Our calling is closely associated with that burden. Rabindranath

Tagore, a Bengali poet, writer, and philosopher, helps to shape this idea. In his poem, Stray Birds, he wrote, *"That which oppresses me, is it my soul trying to come out in the open, or the soul of the world knocking at my heart for its entrance?"*

We cannot escape the depth of our cause. Even if you try to suppress it, there will come a day when an unscripted scenario will pull it out of you. Those around you can sense it and will speak to its unseen potential. There's a reason why you were created and assigned to serve your cause; somebody needs you to show up so they can show up.

So how do you know when you're being pulled to a specific cause? Well, you instantly see a solution to a problem or a way to make it better. While others are paralyzed with doubt and fear, your natural reaction is to move forward into action. Regardless of your status in life, you have particular resources or access to the resources to improve upon a cause that improves humanity's condition. You cannot rest until that issue has either been resolved or at the least significantly addressed.

What would your life look like if you embraced your burden? Who are the people you are assigned to help? What would it take for you to start operating in what you are called to do? Be mindful that you are not going at this alone. You can't complete this mission in your own strength. Knowing the difference between Kingdom Confidence and Carnal Confidence can help you posture your heart so that it's pliable to God's will.

Here's a table that lists a few differences between Carnal Confidence and Kingdom Confidence to help you stay on track. Feel free to make your own table. With the help of Holy Spirit, you will be able to identify even more differences between the two. Post your list in a highly visible area so that you can engage with it regularly.

CARNAL CONFIDENCE Total dependence on you. Proverbs 14:12 (MSG)	KINGDOM CONFIDENCE Total dependence on God Proverbs 3:6 (MSG)
"I am the master of my domain."	"…for it is I who have given you the ability to produce wealth…" Deut. 8:18
"I am smart enough to win on my own."	"Your word is a lamp for my feet, a light on my path." Psalm 119:105
"I have to compete to get all I can right now!"	"…for those who fear Him lack nothing." Psalm 34:9

Imagine you're at the end of your life, and you're looking back. Is there a dream of serving or helping others that would cause you deep regret if you never took the risk to go for it? Your calling is like a magnetic force that will draw people to you when you start walking in it consistently and unashamedly. Contrary to what you've probably been told, they aren't looking for you to be perfect. They prefer you to be real and relatable, a healthy mixture of inspiration and aspiration. People want to be inspired to level up, and at the same time, they need to see and hear your story and aspire to do the same in their life. Paul understood this concept.

He called himself the chief sinner, but he also encouraged the church by sharing his struggle. In Philippians 3:3-9, he delivered so much goodness to the church of Philippi. He said things like:

"For we are the circumcision, the ones who serve by the Spirit of God, boast in Christ Jesus, and do not put confidence in the flesh — although I once also had confidence in the flesh. If anyone else thinks he has grounds for confidence in the flesh, I have more: circumcised the eighth day; of the nation of Israel, of the tribe of Benjamin, a Hebrew born of Hebrews; regarding the law, a Pharisee; regarding zeal, persecuting the church; regarding the righteousness that is in the law, blameless. But everything that was a gain to me, I have considered to be a loss because of Christ. More than that, I also consider everything to be a loss in view of the surpassing value of knowing Christ Jesus my Lord. Because of Him I have suffered the loss of all things and consider them filth, so that I may gain Christ and be found in Him, not having a righteousness of my own from the law, but one that is through faith in Christ — the righteousness from God based on faith. (HCSB)."

Come on! Are you serious, Paul? You consider your gain to be filth? Yep, that's what he said. And he, of all people, had all the right to be self-absorbed. His entire life, leading up to his conversion, was based on cultural and religious confidence. Paul had a privilege. All the amenities of high society were at his fingertips, and he could use that to complete a kingdom agenda.

His burning bush moment happened on the road to Damascus as he was actively engaged in killing Christians, and he kept that fire in his heart and used the tools he already possessed to teach and inspire believers to remain encouraged. In today's context, we would say he had transferable skills.

I believe that the anointing that moved Paul abides in you. Although your paths may not be the same, the impact can be just as big! The sound of you working in your assignment can resonate throughout generations. It could be the very thing that leads someone to embrace the abundant life that Christ died for them to have.

A Prayer for Purpose & Assignment

Father, I open my ears to Your assignment for my life. Show me Your good and perfect will. Help me see the connection between my experiences, what You've called me to do, and who You've called me to serve. You have given me a burden for a specific cause, and I will walk in Kingdom Confidence to demonstrate Your will. Amen

Reflection Questions

If you need more space to record your thoughts, feel free to use the chapter journal in the back of this book.

1. What assignment have you been called to?

2. What transformational tasks/causes are you ignoring or running away from? Why?

3. What needs have you encountered in life that you'd jump at the chance to meet on a larger scale?

Chapter 2

Grow Your Confidence

"For I know the plans I have for you," declares the LORD,
"plans to prosper you and not to harm you,
plans to give you hope and a future."

Jeremiah 29:11

As a kid, one of the most important things for me to do was serving in my church. No one had to force me to do it. I can remember sitting in the church pews watching the adults operate in their gifts and wanted to do it too. The rule in our church was that you couldn't serve in ministry until you were baptized. Baptism was like a rite of passage, and it signified that you were serious about "serving the Lord." So once I turned 12 years old, my Father baptized me, and then I instantly went into ministerial training.

I accepted every opportunity to serve that was available to me, from ushering, leading songs, videotaping the services, serving food during church meals, learning how to prepare and serve communion, and even reading scripture during Sunday morning worship. I didn't shy away from any of it. I loved doing the work, and I thrived in it. I was a teenage boy with teenage tendencies learning how to serve in adult ministry. Thankfully, I had men and women who were patient with me. But there was one situation that bruised my confidence and planted a seed inside of me that took me over 30 years to uproot.

A Seed of Rejection

Within our denomination my home church was known for having some of the best gospel concerts in the metro-Detroit area. It seemed like every other month we were hosting a program where singing groups from all over southeast Michigan would come to perform and fellowship. So I and my two brothers, and three of my cousins thought it would be a good idea to form a singing group so that we could be included on the roster. We were all under the age of fourteen. Our voices were still developing, and our haircuts were atrocious. Now and then, I look at the old VHS footage of us singing and cringe because we were not good at all, but we enjoyed it!

During one of these storied programs, one of the men who I highly respected got on the microphone and made a joke about our group, and the audience laughed. I'm sure to him it was harmless, but it rocked my world. It caused me to feel less than valued. I felt rejected. From that point on, I don't remember serving in the freedom I once had. There was anxiety attached to everything I did. I was afraid of messing up or disappointing people. I would over-prepare to the point that I would have a negative physical reaction when it was time to perform. On the flip side, sometimes I would over-give to cover up the places where I felt empty. I didn't want to seem incompetent, so I wouldn't talk much unless I was asked a question, and even then, I tried to frame my words in a way that didn't offend anyone.

This was my pattern for over 30 years. Still, I didn't know that I was doing it until God exposed it through a conversation I had with a close mentor who gave me some honest feedback during a regular cordial conversation via email. The emotion I felt when I read her words, and my response to her feedback caused me to stop and check myself. I didn't like how I felt. At that time, I didn't know why I responded the way that I did, so I started digging, and it led me back to the incident that happened at my church over 30 years prior.

Once I identified the root of the issue, God revealed that I was dealing with the spirit of rejection. He began to show me how, over the years, I had sabotaged fruitful opportunities because of it. He exposed the areas where I needed to embrace healing and walked with me as I discovered what that looked like. During the process, I learned how the spirit of rejection could derail a person's life if it is not addressed effectively. As I discovered how rejection manifested in my life, I began to feel liberated.

Not because I felt totally free from it at that point, but because now I knew what it was, I was more aware of the triggers, and I was moved to search for strategies to live in that awareness and how to *respond* when I saw and felt the triggers versus *react* to them. Responding and reacting are not the same. A response requires careful consideration and a mature reply free of contempt. A reaction is an emotional, instinctive reply that is self-preserving and defensive. For me, deliverance is more of a journey than a singular event. There is power in knowing about my flaws because it is through God that I'm made strong in my weaknesses. And you are too! (But you already knew that).

Here's what I learned about how the spirit of rejection can influence a person's life. I'm sure there is more fruit, but these are the ones that were demonstrated in my life:

Rejection will cause you to overdo it.
You want to be seen as an overachiever so that your weak areas aren't exposed, or you don't look small.

Rejection will cause you to overshare.
You overshare because you want to make sure people know that your intentions are pure. You attempt to get ahead of their judgment of you to try and circumvent any rejection that could "possibly" come your way.

Rejection will cause you to shrink back.
You've been rejected in the past, and you don't want to feel that pain again, so you'd rather play small than stand out.

Rejection will cause you to be defensive.
You aren't open to healthy correction because someone abused their authority and broke you down in the past.

Rejection will cause you to hide.
You see a problem you can solve, but you won't step up because you believe you're not good enough to execute the solution.

As you learn how to overcome rejection, I encourage you to embrace the feeling and emotion for what it is. Be honest with yourself. Be ok with saying, "I'm feeling rejected because_____ (fill in the blank)." Replace your feelings with words of faith. Verbalize this statement, "I feel rejected because_____ (fill in the blank). But God says_____ (fill in the blank)." Believe what God says about you; if you like music, practice praise, and worship therapy. Listen to music that confirms what God says about you. When you spend time in prayer, repeat God's word in your prayers. When you pray, say, "God, Your word says; _____ (fill in the blank)."

These are just a few ways to remind me that I am healed, and I don't feel the need to hold on to brokenness anymore. This is called activating your confidence. It involves identifying your own limiting beliefs, where they come from, and managing how you respond to them when you are confronted with them. Just like a chiropractor uses the Activator Method's controlled force to target specific joints, you can use this method to target this specific area to activate healing in your life. Through this exercise, I learned that there are levels to overcoming rejection and growing my kingdom confidence, which helps me remain accountable to the truth of this process.

The 4 Levels of Kingdom Confidence

The first level of kingdom confidence is called *Revealed Confidence*. Revealed Confidence is when we can **_sense_** Holy Spirit, and He points us in the direction of God's best for us. We receive divine instruction to accomplish an earthly assignment that has eternal implications.

The second is *Increased Confidence*. At this level, we willingly **_submit_** to the leading of Holy Spirit. Despite the uncertainty, we move forward because we know that Holy Spirit's job is to tell us God's will for us at the moment and for the rest of our lives.

The third is *Validated Confidence*. This is where God **_show's up_** (performs/responds) on behalf of our obedience. He can do whatever He wants when He wants, but He delights in executing His promises. Our obedience gives Him permission and the room to do the exceedingly and abundantly more. His tangible, transformative, and measurable results offer the validation we need to be confident.

Lastly is *Sustained Confidence*. We must **_stay_** in relationship with Him. The relationship is better than a reward. Through the relationship, we are exposed to unfair, unseen, and undiscovered advantages. The relationship gives us access to knowledge and resources that we didn't have to work, hustle, and grind for. Sustained Confidence requires us to develop a relationship routine of prayer, reading the word of God, meditating on the word of God, and applying the word of God to our lives. This routine helps us to remain open to the leading of the Holy Spirit.

Embrace Your Worth

We often limit what we can accomplish, who we can be, and how far we can go. Sometimes those limits indicate our lack of experience or the absence of exposure and access to resources that can stretch our imagination and galvanize our desired reality. In other cases, those limits are just a projection of what we feel about ourselves versus a reflection of who God says that we are, what we can do, and the distance of our potential. They are rooted in fear, whether it's a fear of success, a fear of failure, a fear of how others might view us, or the fear of just showing up in our authenticity. Limiting beliefs keep us stuck and unproductive.

I don't have to take up space on this page to list examples of what limiting beliefs are; you know what they are for you and how they have affected your life. You hear your voice in your head when it's happening, and you can identify all of the opportunities you have rejected because of it. I use the word "rejected" here instead of "missed" because the opportunity is an invite, and you have the option to accept it or reject it based on what you believe. Limiting beliefs are in direct conflict with God's best for you. You can turn your limiting beliefs into limitless beliefs. You are worthy of living this kind of life. You are worthy because of who you belong to. Feel free to walk in your worthiness and remember who raised you!

"Together with Christ Jesus He also <u>raised us up and seated us in the heavens</u>, so that in the coming ages He might display the immeasurable riches of His grace through His kindness to us in Christ Jesus. For you are saved by grace through faith, and this is not from yourselves; it is God's gift— not from works, so that no one can boast.
For we are His creation, created in Christ Jesus for good works, which God prepared ahead of time so that we should walk in them."
Ephesians 2:6-10 (HCSB)

Commit to the process and the rigor of your development.

"Therefore, since we have been declared righteous by faith, we have peace with God through our Lord Jesus Christ. We have also obtained access through Him by faith into this grace in which we stand, and we rejoice in the hope of the glory of God. And not only that, but we also rejoice in our afflictions, because we know that <u>affliction produces endurance, endurance produces proven character, and proven character produces hope</u>. This hope will not disappoint us, because God's love has been poured out in our hearts through the Holy Spirit who was given to us."
Romans 5:1-5 (HCSB)

In this passage, affliction denotes, an internal pressure that causes you to be restricted. It feels like you have no way to escape. You are literally mentally between a rock and a hard place. What I've learned about growing through affliction is that it prepares me for God's next move in my life. Overcoming affliction produces a battle scar that certifies my purpose and assignment. It validates that I have what it takes to do this work, and it assures me that I'm not doing it alone. In that, I can be confident, and I find my worth. My friend, I encourage you to push through whatever your affliction is. Commit to the challenge of being made for this work that you've been called and assigned to. If God didn't trust you to do it, He wouldn't have called you to it.

A Prayer for Kingdom Confidence

Father, Your word says that I am more than a conqueror, and through the power of contentment, I can do all things through Christ, which strengthens me. Show me what Your best looks like for me. I will apply Your word to calibrate my beliefs to Your expectations. Lord, may Your grace reign in my life. Amen

Reflection Questions

If you need more space to record your thoughts, feel free to use the chapter journal in the back of this book.

1. What would your life look like if you decided that you were worthy enough to pursue God's best for you? What kind of parent, employee, spouse, and friend would you be?

2. Review the 4 Levels of Kingdom Confidence. Which one(s) speak to where you are right now and why? Which one(s) do you have to grow into?

3. What limiting beliefs are holding you back from being the best version of yourself?

Chapter 3

The Power of Contentment

Don't worry about anything; instead, pray about everything.
Tell God what you need, and thank him for all he has done.
Then you will experience God's peace, which exceeds
anything we can understand. His peace will guard your
hearts and minds as you live in Christ Jesus. And now, dear
brothers and sisters, one final thing. Fix your thoughts on
what is true, and honorable, and right, and pure, and lovely,
and admirable. Think about things that are excellent and
worthy of praise.

Philippians 4:6-8 (NLT)

I decided to open this chapter with this scripture because I wanted to set the tone for what you are about to read. When I study this passage, it just seems to be the epitome of contentment. No matter what state we're in, Christ is the defender of our hearts. Not our titles, education, or influence but Christ. Contentment comes through knowing Christ, and when we focus our thoughts and actions on Him and exercise thankfulness, we can have peace.

Contentment is defined as a state of happiness and satisfaction. We typically associate contentment with fulfillment, pleasure, cheerfulness, gladness, gratification, restfulness, well-being, peace, serenity, and tranquility. However, the big question is whether we have to work for this or is it readily available to us? As with all things pertaining to life and godliness, the Bible often provides us with the answers we desperately need. Philippians 4:6-7 helps me to remain in a state of contentment.

"Don't be pulled in different directions or worried about a thing. Be saturated in prayer throughout each day, offering your faith-filled requests before God with overflowing gratitude. Tell him every detail of your life, then God's wonderful peace that transcends human understanding will make the answers known to you through Jesus Christ (TPT)."

The 3 Contentment Principles

As God was taking me through my healing process, being content was hard for me to do, and it's still an area that I'm growing in. Then, I was in a space where I just wanted to feel better. I wanted the process to be over, so I would be halfway obedient at times or just doing enough to get by. But looking back, God needed me to stay in the fire of development because He was burning some stuff away and off of me. It was part of the purification process, per se. I had to feel that sting. I couldn't rush through it. So for me not to lose my mind, I *had* to learn how to be content. It wasn't voluntary, but it was necessary! Here are three lessons I learned about being content.

Being content shows that you trust God. When you are at peace, have good pleasure, and are satisfied, it confirms that you believe God to be who He said He is in your life.

You won't be easily shaken by circumstances you have no control over. And even if you did have a sense of control, you have conditioned yourself to ask, "God, what is your best for me in this situation?" And you respond in obedience to what you hear because you trust that His solution is better than any answer you can manufacture.

Being content shows that you are not double-minded. We can trust God when we are in a relationship with Him. Because you trust God, you can focus on His promises instead of your problems. Earlier I shared with you a few principles that can help you overcome the spirit of rejection. One of those principles was to recite the scriptures to yourself to help you believe what God says about you. Even when you don't feel like it, this keeps us focused on a single plan that is doubtless. James 1:7-8 lays out this principle plainly, *"When you are half-hearted and wavering, it leaves you unstable. Can you really expect to receive anything from the Lord when you're in that condition (TPT)?"*

You can't pray about something and then worry at the same time. Those are two competing requests. Yes, worry is a request because you're trying to pull an answer from a source outside yourself. Either you believe that God will answer your prayer the way He desires to, or you believe that you can get to a solution by worrying about it. Whichever thought is the most dominant will win. Whatever you dwell on, that is what you'll do.

You can be content when you have been faithful to the process. I've had to learn the hard way how not to fight the war between faithfulness and perfection. God has not called us to be perfect; He called us to demonstrate our belief in Him by being faithful and obedient. The process of faithfulness doesn't always look pretty. It doesn't always feel good. Like Abraham, sometimes it may look like God is stripping you away from your comfort zone. Like Isaac, God could be asking you to sacrifice a part of yourself that you've invested time, money, and your emotional currency into nurturing. Accepting what seems to be the lesser option can dampen your courage and bruise your ego. But, as with most things God-related, He never asks you to let go of something unless He's provided a better option for you. But you won't even get to see what that is if you aren't faithful to the process to the end.

The disturbing thing about the process is that we don't know what's coming next most of the time. Now, Holy Spirit can help position us for the impact, but that doesn't exempt us from feeling its effects. Though we may feel the tribulation of the test, we can find comfort in knowing that it's only grooming us to walk in God's better option for us. The better option is a reflection of His will. His better option doesn't just satisfy the moment; it has an eternal impact. When you know that you've been faithful to the process, you can be content.

The Benefits of Contentment

Contentment requires us to slow down, align our expectations, and trust that our obedience will yield favorable results. It helps us to see what's truly important, necessary, and vital to our survival. Aligning our expectations helps us to separate fantasy from reality. It allows us to filter out any frivolous options that can rob us of our time and energy. And when we trust the process, it eliminates the pull of our pride to enforce our own solutions. My friend, there are benefits to being content.

You don't feel the need to be involved in everything. When I first started my journey as an author, speaker, and coach, I consumed as much content as possible to help me get to my destination faster. I studied hours of video, listened to countless audio teachings, registered for conferences, bought the books, joined the networking groups, and signed up for hundreds of email lists to get the knowledge I thought I needed. I didn't know it at the time, but I had too many voices vying for my attention. I digested so much information that I got confused. I found myself trying to apply carnal strategies to what was supposed to be a spirit-led business.

As a kingdom-driven entrepreneur, there are some practical business strategies that I just can't ignore, but the majority of my business growth has been the result of divine instruction. Once I began to tap into God's best for my business, I realized that I had too many options on the table. Too many pathways led to nowhere, and too many concepts weren't working for me. I had to offload that baggage and double-down on what truly mattered. During this process, God began to show me what I needed for where I was. Soon I began to notice how lighter I felt. I stopped trying to do everything, and that's when I found contentment.

When you are content, you are cautious with your time. You are a good steward of your energy. The trends of culture and the marketplace don't drive you. Trends are informed by the emotional responses of the industry. People drive industries. So, when people's minds change, the trends change, influencing that industry's economics or culture.

But as believers, we must be vigilant about how we invest our time and where we direct our attention. Are you willing to say no to an opportunity that seems good but is in direct conflict with what you believe? Will you turn down the volume of your core values to gain the affection of those who influence the culture or your industry? In Ephesians 4:11-14, Paul is holding the church at Ephesus accountable for their growth. He reminds them of the assignment of apostles, prophets, evangelists, pastors, and teachers. In addition to that, he also infers that it's possible to be manipulated by the various schools of thought that are not aligned with a kingdom mindset. *"Then we will no longer be immature like children. We won't be tossed and blown about by every wind of new teaching. We will not be influenced when people try to trick us with lies so clever they sound like the truth* (NLT).*"*

If you are involved in everything, how can you be focused on the main thing? At what point does all of your activity become a distraction? Distraction is a trick that the enemy uses to keep us from maximizing our potential. To the person who believes that being busy is equal to being productive, I want to encourage you to ask God what you need to give up. When you practice being content, you are stewarding God's influence in your life. As you commit to being targeted and intentional, God can cause you to be just as effective by doing less.

You are less likely to engage in self-sabotaging behavior. Self-sabotaging behavior is a reflection of how you see yourself. Your self-perception dictates your emotional responses and influences how you engage with the world around you. There are too many self-sabotaging patterns to list, but two examples I'll share here are:

1. Refusing to be aware of your weaknesses.

2. Not feeling worthy.

Not being aware of your weaknesses is dangerous because it can cause you to operate in a capacity you don't have the skillset to perform in. Some of your weaknesses could become a strength if you committed to filling the knowledge gap, but pride won't allow you to be humble enough to submit to being taught something new so you continue to experience subpar results. In terms of worthiness, if you don't think that you deserve something, you will find a way to push it away. Unfortunately, some people go to drastic measures to destroy great opportunities, the same opportunities they cry and pray for. However, as far as kingdom contentment is concerned, the attention is no longer on you but on how God can work *through* you. In that, you become a living sacrifice.

My father once told me that the problem with being a living sacrifice is that we can choose to crawl off the alter whenever the fire gets too hot. If it's not addressed, the spirit of self-sabotaging behavior can be transferred to our children and those who have given us permission to lead them. The seed of self-sabotage can be traced to a traumatic event or learned behavior. It is a means of purpose prevention. Although being delivered from this stronghold can bring glory to God, it is not of God.

You can distinguish good opportunities from God's opportunities. Every good opportunity isn't for you. There is a peace that accompanies God's opportunities, your discernment is heightened, and you are more likely to hear Him clearly and welcome His presence because your gates are open. There are no competing demands, and of course, your ego is in check, and your pride has been diminished. What God wants to do through you is the priority.

Even when it looks like you're getting the short end of the stick, show up in our assignment, and His grace will do the rest; it will carry you. God's grace makes you look better than what you really are. This benefit of contentment will cause you to stay honest about your assignment. You won't chase opportunities that don't belong to you. You will stay in *your* lane and perfect *your* craft. You are less likely to compete with other believers because you've learned there is no competition in the kingdom.

The Enemy of Contentment

Please believe me; the enemy doesn't want you to be content. He wants you to discredit, doubt, and destroy yourself. The antagonist of contentment is worry. Worry is not just a spiritual attack, but it harms you physically. It affects your nervous system by causing it to release stress hormones that speed up your breathing, and raises your blood sugar. It increases your blood pressure and can cause a heart attack or stroke. It also affects your muscles and instigates tension in your neck and shoulders, which leads to migraine headaches. It weakens your immune system, making it hard to fend off colds and the flu.

If contentment weren't important, the enemy wouldn't try so hard to prevent you from discovering your peace. Earlier, we said that worry is a request because it causes you to pull a solution from an outside source. I'm not sure about you, but worrying has never solved a problem in my life. It has never given me the solution that I needed. Worrying has never paid a bill, changed a bad relationship, or helped me do my job better. However, the action of contentment has created waves of peace on many occasions. Contrary to how people may see it, contentment is an active response. So let's address a few misconceptions.

The Misconceptions of Contentment

Misconception 1: *Contentment is the act of settling for less than you deserve.* On the contrary, contentment is your response to God's invitation to rest in Him. When you understand who you're serving, the focus doesn't have to be on what you think you deserve; it's more about what's available to you. We know that God's ways and thoughts supersede any standard we have established for our joy and happiness.

Misconception 2: *Contentment is laziness.* I can see how resting in God can look like doing nothing. When we have subscribed to the proverbial membership of the self-made academy, whose moniker is, "If you're not grinding, you're not growing," it can require us to look "busy" all of the time. I agree with putting forth one's best effort to accomplish a task. I'm all for earning your keep. There's an indescribable pleasure that accompanies a job well done. But what I've found to be true is that we can sometimes base our identity in our work when that honor should be attributed to God.

There will be times when contentment will require you to scale back on your efforts. And it will appear that less work is being done on your behalf. But contentment doesn't advocate for inactivity. Conversely, your movement and pursuit are spirit-led. It's purposeful and meaningful. And God can respond to your obedience in a way that outmatches your performance.

Misconception 3: *Contentment is a weak response to being challenged.* We are faced with challenges every day. Some of those challenges stir up the gift inside of us and push us into a new level of thinking. These challenges activate and ignite an immediate response that gives us insight into who we really are. But not every challenge needs an immediate response. There's an art to knowing how and when to respond to a challenge, offense, or test. Being content helps you discern whether or not you're supposed to respond at all, and if you are, what the proper response should be. To see this principle in action, we can look at the examples set before us.

"The words of the reckless pierce like swords, but the tongue of the wise brings healing (Proverbs 12:18). *"*

"This you know, my beloved brethren. But everyone must be quick to hear, slow to speak and slow to anger; for the anger of man does not achieve the righteousness of God (James 1:19, NASB 1995). *"*

"Those who guard their mouths and their tongues keep themselves from calamity (Proverbs 21:23). *"*

The value of contentment has been lost on the seemingly permanent face-paced reality of our culture. The speed of *now* has weakened the effectiveness of patience, and the pressure that often accompanies convenience can dilute the potency of longsuffering. So, we must not forget that the presence of contentment does not mean a lack of pleasure. It affirms our devotion to the one who gives us satisfaction, the source of our fulfillment, and the author of our peace.

A Prayer For Contentment

Father, Your word says that You will keep me in perfect peace when my mind stays on You. Help me to filter out thoughts that don't align with Your will for me. I declare that the enemy's schemes will not shake me, and I will not be pressured to perform on behalf of my pride. I will rest in You. Amen

Reflection Questions

If you need more space to record your thoughts, feel free to use the chapter journal in the back of this book.

1. Think about a time when you weren't content. What events led up to your discontentment?

2. How do you respond when you are not at peace?

3. Review the benefits of contentment that were listed in this chapter. Which one(s) resonate with you the most? Why?

Chapter 4

The Challenge of Certainty

"Trust in the LORD with all your heart and lean not on your own understanding; in all your ways submit to him, and he will make your paths straight."

Proverbs 3:5-6

Up until now, you've learned that you've been called to accomplish a specific assignment. You've also been exposed to the various Kingdom Confidence levels and learned that you are indeed worthy of your calling. In the previous chapter, you read about the benefits of being content. If you haven't already experienced it, you're going to be tested. The question will evolve from, "What do I need to know?" to "Do I believe what I already know?" You're going to shift from the *knowledge accumulation* phase to the *application of information* stage.

Right now, it's not about reacting to what's happening around you; it's about your response-ability. Meaning, when your test arrives, do you have the tools and discipline (ability) to respond accordingly? Arriving at a place of certainty is not easy. Certainty is a combination of Trust + Discipline. Trust is the firm belief in the reliability of someone or something. Discipline is simply your ability to control your behavior.

Do You Have The Courage to Be Certain?

The evidence of your certainty is when you can relinquish your plan & willingly submit to His. Sometimes, our agenda is informed by our past trauma, our education, or some other creative fallible system that will eventually crumble in the presence of God. God's plan encompasses every part of your life. He has a plan for your family, marriage, business, church, etc. He wants to give you His best in every area of your life that you willingly give Him access to. So when you say, "God, take it. Do what you will," that's an indication that you've entered into His rest.

A courageous certainty says that even when you are not confident in your ability, you are certain that God is in control. Your belief is firm because you know that God is reliable. Certainty requires you to be still, even when your trust is tested. Your certainty will come under fire. Your confidence is heavily dependent on the H2MF Rule: Heart, Head, Mouth, and Feet. Whatever you believe in your heart, you will dwell on. Whatever you dwell on will come out of your mouth. Whatever you say will eventually be the direction in which you move.

Your Assignment Is Bigger Than Your WHY

In 2010, Simon Sinek shook up the world when he did a TED Talk that challenged leaders to "start with why." His influence caused people to find their "why" or their reason for playing big in their respective lives. Essentially they are asking, "What is the single, most urgent, and important reason for all of my life's activity?" Permit me to challenge that philosophy. Your Kingdom assignment is more important than your WHY. Take a few seconds to process what you just read.

I believe that Simon's concept has awakened millions of people to the possibility of living a meaningful life. However, I submit to you that for the last ten years, we've been asking for the answer to a question that moves with life's circumstances. Instead we should be asking, "What is my assignment?" When you know what that is, you can be certain that the results of your obedience to your assignment will be far greater than whatever your "why" can produce.

Don't underestimate the power of leaning into this. In chapter one we determined that your purpose is "why you were created," but your assignment is *how* you demonstrate it in various environments. You can know your purpose and still not be in purpose. You can have clarity of your "why" and still not be as effective as you should be. Your assignment encompasses obedience + action. When you are in your assignment, it gives life to your purpose because that's when you can identify purpose in every part of your life.

My purpose in life is to encourage and equip leaders to become the better version of themselves, which is the reflection of Christ. But how do I demonstrate that in every area of my life? Well, as a father, I demonstrate that by creating environments where my children can thrive and feel safe. As a husband, I demonstrate it by expressing my love for my wife, respecting her, supporting her interest and encouraging her to cultivate her gifts. As a business leader, I demonstrate that by helping my clients grow their faith as they grow their business. As a civic leader, I demonstrate that by partnering with schools and organizations to teach the youth how to lead unapologetically in their sphere of influence.

Our "why" speaks to how *we* want to show up in the world. Our assignment speaks to how *God* needs us to represent the kingdom. Our purpose is all about awareness and identity, but our assignment is about action. It puts a seed in the ground. When you understand that your assignment is bigger than your why, that, as Robert Fulgham stated, "Changes the focus from me to the kingdom."

Certainty Requires You to Be Still

Being still doesn't suggest that you are doing nothing. It means that you won't abandon your assignment. A great example of this is the relationship between David and Saul. After Saul was rejected as king, he developed vicious hate towards David. After several death attempts on his life, David decided to go on the run and remove himself from Saul's reach and influence. But Saul didn't necessarily agree with David's point of view. He hunted David down with the intent to kill him on sight. David had every right to defend himself against Saul's murderous threats. Still, David remained in a position of honor and refrained from killing a king even though he had several opportunities to do it. He knew his time to reign was near.

In 1 Samuel 24:1-13, Saul was told where David was located. So he gathered a search party of three thousand elite military men to go and capture David. During the journey, Saul had to use the bathroom, so he relieved himself in a cave. What he didn't know was that he chose the very cave David and his men were hiding in. David's men got excited and said, *"This is the day the Lord spoke of when he said to you, 'I will give your enemy into your hands for you to deal with as you wish* (verse 4). '"

David then had a moment of revenge because he crept up unnoticed and cut off a corner of Saul's robe. But he soon felt remorse, and his conscience wouldn't let him boast at that moment. He said to his men, *"'The Lord forbid that I should do such a thing to my master, the Lord's anointed, or lay my hand on him; for he is the anointed of the Lord." With these words David sharply rebuked his men and did not allow them to attack Saul. And Saul left the cave and went his way* (verse 6-7)."

In 1 Samuel 26, again, we see Saul's disdain for David. Once Saul found out where David was, he put together an army of three thousand men to search for him. He set up camp near David's location and secured his position. David found out that Saul was in his vicinity and waited until nightfall to make his move.

"Then David set out and went to the place where Saul had camped. He saw where Saul and Abner son of Ner, the commander of the army, had lain down. Saul was lying inside the camp, with the army encamped around him...So David and Abishai went to the army by night, and there was Saul, lying asleep inside the camp with his spear stuck in the ground near his head. Abner and the soldiers were lying around him. Abishai said to David, "Today God has delivered your enemy into your hands. Now let me pin him to the ground with one thrust of the spear; I won't strike him twice." But David said to Abishai, "Don't destroy him! Who can lay a hand on the Lord's anointed and be guiltless? As surely as the Lord lives," he said, "the Lord himself will strike him, or his time will come and he will die, or he will go into battle and perish. But the Lord forbid that I should lay a hand on the Lord's anointed. Now get the spear and water jug that are near his head, and let's go (verses 5, 8-11)."

David was certain his time to reign was near. He was confident in his assignment, so when he could've killed Saul in the cave and at Saul's campsite, he stood still.

Perfect opportunities are not always purposeful opportunities. In what area of your life and business are you anxious to make a move based on the circumstances happening around you? When we are shaken by what we think are immediate demands, we can unknowingly shift the balance of favor. Like David, when you know your assignment, you will not allow circumstances to disrupt the rhythm of your obedience.

Your Certainty Will Come Under Fire

As you are building up your sensitivity to certainty, your faith will be challenged. Distractions can arise out of nowhere. Being entertained by things that no longer serve you will keep you out of alignment with God's will. This is where discipline comes in. You will learn how to hear and sense the shift in your spirit.

There was a period in my life when I was distracted by good things, but that good activity kept me from elevating to the place that God needed me to be. During this time I was on the board of a prestigious non-profit organization that was doing great work in my community. The president of that organization mentored me, and I made a few strategic connections to help my professional career. But after a few years of service, I began to feel a tug.

I didn't know what it was, but I sensed a shift, and the feeling rested on my heart for some time. I tried to ignore it because I thought being connected to this organization was an opportunity to further my career and get access to the resources that I'd been searching for, but I couldn't shake the divine sensation to move. It didn't leave. Eventually, I decided to yield to the tugging in my spirit, and that's when I heard God say, "Start clearing your plate."

I then scheduled a meeting with my mentor to tell him that I would resign from my seat on the board. After our meeting, I felt a weight lift off my shoulder. The interesting part about it is that I didn't even know the weight was there. It's funny how we can carry something that feels like an opportunity, but it's actually a weight. After feeling that freedom, I began to ask God if there was anything else I was carrying that I should to surrender. He began to reveal other areas in my life where I needed to clear my table. From throwing away items in my home, to monitoring my relationships, to addressing a few internal issues preventing me from living in His unforced rhythm. The more I was obedient to clearing my table, the more liberated I felt. I had to move those things so that He could have room to work in my life. But this didn't come easy. There was a lot of resistance.

The Resistance Factor

Once you've committed to certainty and decided to move forward in your assignment, at some point in time, you will encounter resistance in three major areas: Internal Resistance, External Resistance, and Spiritual Resistance. They may not happen in this sequence, but they will eventually show up in your life in some way or another.

Internal Resistance happens when God reveals the broken places He wants to mend, but your flesh fights the process. God doesn't expose you to hurt you; He's just preparing you to be a good steward of your table. When I discovered that I was being challenged in the area of rejection, my flesh tried to fight the process. I was appalled at the thought of that spirit having a resting place inside of me. Over time, I learned that God was not trying to shine a light on my incompetence; He was instead showing me how to do the work to get better in that area so that I could help someone else. I was responsible for how long I allowed my flesh to reject this evolution. The length of time we experience this internal resistance is contingent upon us yielding to the progressive will of God for us.

External Resistance can occur when you become more disciplined with your time and intentional in your assignment. You may experience a protest from those around you, and soon you could begin to feel the distance between you and them. In terms of this separation, there can be a ripping away of sorts or a gradual disengagement. In some cases, the grievance might be malicious, but not all situations are like this. When people get to know you at one level, they can claim ownership of you at that level, and it may be hard for them to relate to your growth. So to keep you close, they may be reluctant to support your growth because it can threaten their relationship with you. I know that can be a lot to take in. But when your level of certainty increases and you begin living in your transformation, you'll start to sense who is equipped to accompany you and who isn't.

When I was in high school, I was the only one out of all my friends who had access to a vehicle. My parents allowed me to drive their car every now and then, but their only rule was to make sure the car had gas in it when I brought it back home. All of my friends knew that if they were going to ride with me, they had to pitch in on the gas money. One day, we all decided to play basketball at the community center, and I was slated to drive us there. Everyone agreed to contribute to the trip, except one person. He vehemently refused to help out with gas. Consequently, he was left behind. As you grow into the knowledge of your assignment, you will find that some people can't fuel your mission. Everybody can't ride with you. This is not to hold them in contempt; it's not a good person vs. bad person type of scenario. However, your certainty in God calls for you to stay true to managing God's influence in your life, regardless of the external resistance.

Spiritual Resistance occurs when there is a conflict between our current religious beliefs and the truth of God's reality. Keep in mind that the source of this conflict might look different for each of us. Once I began learning about the kingdom, I found that the doctrine I had been taught as a kid had holes in it that could only be sealed up with God's grace.

As a child, I was trained, whether directly or indirectly, that my particular denomination was where God lived and that everyone else was in error. This message was somehow infused into every act of service that we did, and if we dared to rebel against it, we'd be subject to the wrath of God and disassociated from the fellowship. When it came to having a relationship with Him, I felt that God was like a monster in heaven waiting to pounce on me whenever I did something wrong. I don't recall learning about the power of His grace or the depths of His love.

As a young adult, I intentionally began my journey to figure out who God is to me and what made all of these denominations different. When I got to college, I purposely visited as many diverse churches as I could. Through this journey, God slowly unraveled what our relationship could be. Through that, I discovered that He didn't hate the other denominations; we just expressed our gratitude to Him differently. But what made us the same was that we recognized that Jesus was the standard for whom we can all look to. The blood was the connecting agent between us all.

I soon found myself getting angry for all the years I "wasted" in such a suffocating system. I held contempt in my heart towards those who had taught me a way of life that limited me. Therein lays another conflict because I loved these people. They invested in me, and their influence helped me walk in my purpose before knowing what it was. I knew they loved God, yet, I felt manipulated. But God began to work on my heart concerning that contempt. I still had to honor them. My prayers became more intentional and purposeful around this matter, and hearing from Holy Spirit became paramount. I needed it to be.

Soon, that contempt transformed into pity, then to love, and eventually grace. The grace that God showed me I now had to extend to my teachers and those who influenced my spiritual growth as a youth. So today, when I go back and visit the church I grew up in, I can embrace the experience for what it is, and I can honor those who laid the foundation for my spiritual growth. The purpose of spiritual resistance is to recalibrate your total man. In this, Mark 12:30 will come alive for you, *"Love the Lord your God with all your heart and with all your soul and with all your mind and with all your strength."*

The challenge of certainty will look and feel different for each of us. The test will prompt you to respond, and your response will be a reflection of what's already on the inside of you.

A Prayer For Certainty

Father, in the midst of all that is going on around me, I will trust You and remain disciplined to who You called me to be. Your word is a lamp to my feet and a light unto my path. When I experience resistance, I will not resist You. I know that being in a relationship with You gives me an unfair advantage. And I am certain that You know what's best for me. Amen.

Reflection Questions

If you need more space to record your thoughts, feel free to use the chapter journal in the back of this book.

1. In what area of your life are you currently being challenged to trust God in? How have you responded?

2. When you review the Resistance Factor, which level of resistance resonates with you the most? Why?

3. How have you been challenged to be still? What has been your response?

Chapter 5

You've Been Charged

"Go, stand in the temple courts," he said,
"and tell the people all about this new life."

Acts 5:20

Webster defines charge as the ability to entrust (someone) with a task as a duty or responsibility. In the context of Kingdom Confidence, the purpose of a charge is to establish you as an evangelistic voice to ignite the body of Christ like only you can. God has given you a message to share, and you are responsible for sharing it, sharing it often, sharing it with confidence, and making sure that message points back to Jesus.

Share The Message, Share It Often, and Share it With Confidence.

Sharing your message is one of the most effective ways to demonstrate Kingdom Confidence, but what does it mean, and what does it look like? Your message is the testament of your transformation. It is your evidence of God's goodness. It includes your authentic journey of growth, what you've learned along the way, and how you can look back and identify God's hand in the process.

Be spirit-led in your approach. Be wise about the motive behind sharing your message. Are you doing it to get attention? Are you using your message to manipulate people into following you or buying from you? Are you looking for sympathy, or is your motive to help someone? Your message is someone else's solution. Use every platform that is available to you to evangelize about your transformation. Be consistent in sharing it because the more you share it, the more proficient you will get at sharing it. As a result, your confidence will grow.

I had a client who wanted to write a book about an experience she went through. She was a highly educated woman and was accomplished in her profession, but in terms of publishing a book she didn't know where to start. During one of our coaching sessions, I gave her a homework assignment. She was to record a 10-minute live video on one of her social media pages talking about some of the content she was writing in her book. The only caveat was to ask Holy Spirit what she needed to say. She was petrified of doing this and put up a great amount of resistance. It took me some time to convince her that what I was asking of her could add value to those following her pages. I assured her that the video didn't have to be perfect; she just needed to be authentic and talk about her journey.

She did the assignment, and the response was overwhelming. From that experience, she discovered that people were attracted to her authenticity, and they related to her struggle more than she expected. She was so encouraged by the response that she recorded a few more videos without me telling her to. As a result of her stepping out and sharing her story more, she received over 100 pre-orders of her book in less than 30 days. Not too long after her first release, she launched her second book and used that same spirit-led approach to reach the people who valued her story.

You have the life experience, and nobody can dispute what you've overcome. So, share the message when people want to hear it and when they don't. Share it in love. When the message points back to the cross, it takes the pressure off of you to perform.

The Benefits of Your Charge

As you share the message, you will find that God's work is being done at multiple levels. He can get more done through your obedience than you can do through developing any strategy or campaign on your own. It opens up a world of opportunity for you to glorify God and touch the lives of those you've been assigned to. Here are just a few benefits to being faithful to your charge.

You Will Fulfill The Greater Works

Those who believe in Christ can do the work that He did and more. Unapologetically sharing your message will contribute to kingdom work being done. And when we live in that space, God's response is favorable on behalf of our requests. John 14:12-13 outlines the validity of this thought.

"Very truly I tell you, whoever believes in me will do the works I have been doing, and they will do even greater things than these because I am going to the Father. And I will do whatever you ask in my name, so that the Father may be glorified in the Son."

Your Obedience To The Charge
Has Eternal Implications

The charge to share your message is deeper than you can imagine. Who knows what can happen when you share the message that God has developed on the inside of you. That message can permeate throughout generations. Once released, it is like a fragrance that lingers in the air of time, and those who need it will find it.

My mother once shared a truth with me that helped change my perspective on the work I was doing in the area of youth leadership. At one point, I was growing weary in my work. It just seemed as if the reward wasn't matching all of the time I was putting in. She reminded me that even though I couldn't see the reward just yet, the seed that I was planting could start to blossom years from now. "Just imagine if one of your young men was chosen for a job interview," she said. "The principles you taught him in your program could help him land that job. Teaching him how to tie a tie might be the very thing he needed to boost his confidence to apply for that position. And because you taught him that one act of grooming, he can now teach his son, and the cycle will continue." Something as simple as sharing your message could impact the lives of several generations and beyond.

Committing to the Charge Produces
Equitable & Sustainable Fruit

In John 15:16, Jesus said, *"You did not choose me, but I chose you and appointed you so that you might go and bear fruit—fruit that will last—and so that whatever you ask in my name the Father will give you."* The Greek translation for "fruit" in this context is *karpos:* everything done in true partnership with Christ. It results from two life streams-the Lord living His life through ours-to yield what is eternal

(HELPS Word-studies). This description is consistent with what Jesus said in verse 4, *"No branch can bear fruit by itself; it must remain in the vine. Neither can you bear fruit unless you remain in me."*

This fruit is directly correlated with God's greater work that was prepared for us to do at the beginning of time. It is the fruit that was determined in eternity *for* eternity's sake. God's charge on your life brings stability of purpose. Though you may not know every step, that's where faith comes in. God is nonpartisan in His approach; He responds to obedience or the lack thereof. In our quest for independence, our flesh can cause us to believe we are the master of our domain. How can this be when the earth is the Lord's?

Let us not forget that we are not in control. The fruit that we attempt to produce on our own will spoil because our power is limited to our ability to see what's next. And at our best, what we see can only be a prediction based on past trends and results. Although that data is an indicator of what could happen, it's not substantial. God delights in performing His promises. He's not concerned about what He can get *from* you, but what He can get *to* you. And the fruit of that relationship will continue to produce more than your work can yield.

Remaining Faithful to the Charge Builds Your Kingdom Credibility

In an attempt to restore the relationship between Philemon and his servant, Onesimus, the Apostle Paul highlighted Philemon's reputation and his devotion to Christ and the saints that met in his home.

"I always thank my God when I mention you in my prayers, because I hear of your love and faith toward the Lord Jesus

and for all the saints. I pray that your participation in the faith may become effective through knowing every good thing that is in us for the glory of Christ. For I have great joy and encouragement from your love, because the hearts of the saints have been refreshed through you, brother (Philemon 1:4-7, HCSB).*"*

There was no social media back then. No telephones. No instant way to communicate with those who weren't in your immediate vicinity. They had letters and word of mouth. That's it. So Philemon's reputation of integrity, faith, and love is what gave him influence with Paul. Like Philemon, your faithfulness to your charge builds your credibility. Director and writer Stephen King said, "We never know which lives we influence, or when, or why." You don't get to choose how you influence people or how deep the influence runs; your responsibility is to stay focused on the charge placed on your life.

In John 4:1-42, we are granted exclusive access into the encounter the Samaritan woman had with Jesus at Jacobs Well. After He ministered to her, she ran and shared her transformation with the people who were in her immediate network. As a result of her sharing her message, people believed in Jesus and were thirsty for their own encounter.

"So when the Samaritans came to him, they urged him to stay with them, and he stayed two days. And because of his words many more became believers. They said to the woman, "We no longer believe just because of what you said; now we have heard for ourselves, and we know that this man really is the Savior of the world."

When we share our message, it's as if God is lending us His influence. And how we manage it is a reflection of our reverence towards Him. When our motives are rooted in love, the aroma of Christ will capture the hearts of the willing. So, being mindful of the challenges of your charge is necessary.

Outside influences and authority figures that teach strategies contrary to God's word can be a major distraction. Especially when they have the apparent success that you desire to have. Who are you listening to, who has your ear, your heart, and your mind? Who has your undivided attention? Why are you following them? Do they have sustainable fruit, or does their message change with the demand of the marketplace? Who you listen to determines what you do and informs your credibility.

Pride and entitlement are a few other detractors. When you feel like you're too big to share your message, or you've determined that your message is better than someone else's you are essentially trying to undermine their effectiveness. This, my friend, is a heart issue. You claim a "lane," and if anyone else's message resembles that lane, you feel the need to compete with them versus collaborate with them. Be careful of allowing pride and entitlement to creep in, for they are forms of destruction and an act of abandonment that can cause you to become inconsistent and entangled in perfectionism.

Your message isn't even about you, but God can use you to get His message out. Like the Samaritan woman, the charge on your life is the meeting place for God's grace and your deficiencies. Together they form a bond that creates a sweet-smelling fragrance that heaven acknowledges as a sacrifice.

A Prayer For Your Charge

Father, You've called me to go into all the world, and You've equipped me with the tools to share my message of transformation with boldness. The harvest is readily available. And I declare that as I go forth in Your power and authority, the fruit that is produced will live forever, and Your name will be glorified. Amen.

Reflection Questions

If you need more space to record your thoughts, feel free to use the chapter journal in the back of this book.

1. Review this chapter and share the part you identify with the most and why.

2. What is your message, and why are you the one to share it?

3. How does your message glorify God? How is it a reflection of Christ? Is it drawing all men to you, or Jesus?

Chapter 6

The Wave of Consistency

"Therefore, my dear brothers and sisters, stand firm. Let nothing move you. Always give yourselves fully to the work of the Lord, because you know that your labor in the Lord is not in vain."

1 Corinthians 15:58

Some choose to live their lives by the roll of the dice. They've put their destiny into the hands of chance. Thus, submitting to its consequences and relinquishing all control to the uncertainty of the roll. Even more, some have become devout disciples of unending, unearned leisure. Maximizing every opportunity to contribute a minor investment, yet they expect a major return. They have eliminated sacrifice from their equation of personal and spiritual success.

These attitudes support a dangerous philosophy that leads to destruction and decreases the value of consistency over time. Consistency is defined as an agreement or harmony of parts or features to one another or a whole (Webster

Merriam). Looking further at this meaning, I'm reminded of how Paul describes the body of Christ in 1 Corinthians 12:12-27: *"For just as the body is one and has many members, and all the members of the body, though many, are one body, so it is with Christ...If one member suffers, all suffer together; if one member is honored, all rejoice together* (ESV)."

What an amazing picture of what consistency looks like and what it can be. Physically, every part of the body is informed by another part of the body. They feed off of one another. With you demonstrating the power, authority, and influence of God in your life and business, every part of you contributes to this being your reality.

Consistency can be elusive at times. To stay the course and devote intentional energy towards a purpose is an ever-present battle. One could speculate about why a person struggles to be consistent; I would be hard-pressed to list them all here. But what I'm sure of is there is no magic pill to help remedy this. But if consistency is the agreement or harmony of parts to one another, I submit to you that, at the root, we struggle with consistency because there could be a disconnection between our mind, body, and spirit that can cause an imbalance of movement. That disconnect contributes to unstable behaviors that are driven by our emotions and unproductive desires.

Entrepreneur and writer Maria Forleo said: "Success doesn't come from what you do occasionally, it comes from what you do consistently." As I'm writing this, there were days when I loathed the thought of sitting at the computer to type these words. I knew I wanted to complete this book within a specific timeframe, but there were days when I'd rather be sitting on the couch watching a good documentary while eating a bowl of cereal. Now, I did indulge a few times during the process. But too much leisure time would've prevented me from meeting my writing goal within the intended timeframe. So when I felt the arms of comfort trying to embrace me, I resisted and reset my affection on the goal at hand. There are a few basic pieces to the framework of kingdom consistency that keep me alert when I want to do otherwise.

Components of Kingdom Consistency

Godly assurance is an element of kingdom consistency. Learning happens when there is a rub between who we are and who God designed us to be. It's a matter of confrontation versus retreat. We can either confront our current reality or retreat from it. However, confrontation can be a beautiful opportunity for us to actualize the knowledge of Christ in us. This is not always an easy process, but God is trying to develop us to build us up. And we can be assured that it's for our good and the greater good of the kingdom.

Self-assurance is yet another element of kingdom consistency. It is developed in the course of doing. Our faith grows when we apply the knowledge that comes through obedience, and we commit to the rigor of development. You can be poised as God is expanding your capacity.

NBA legend, Kobe Bryant, was once interviewed about his mental toughness. The interviewer asked how he could remain focused during crunch time and other high-pressure game-time situations. Kobe responded by saying that he practiced at game speed. He simulated real game situations during his workouts to build up his pressure tolerance. So when he was in those situations during a real game, his mind and body didn't know the difference because he was so used to practicing with that level of intensity.

Taking Kobe's mindset into account and leaning on the biblical pillar of 1 Corinthians 15:58, we can see that self-assurance and poise grow when we commit ourselves fully to the work that we've been assigned to complete.

Godly assurance and self-assurance can prepare us for marketplace assurance. When you show up consistently, the market responds. There are people leading successful businesses right now because they refused to give up. Individuals who may not appear to be as talented or intelligent as the majority, but they have committed to the pathway of process and are seeing results. They understand that properly applied repetition creates positive momentum. And as they share their message, they become more refined in their presentation, and those who need what they have will reward that consistency with their attention and resources.

So although the market trends don't dictate our faith, consistency puts us in a position to ride the wave of momentum when the market calls. Momentum can't be packaged and sold. It's not something you can fabricate. It doesn't occur just because you thought about it. Consistency attracts momentum.

Business philosopher Jim Rohn said, "Success is neither magical nor mysterious. Success is the natural consequence of consistently applying fundamentals." Your credibility increases when your values and actions are uniform. People will permit you to lead them when you have demonstrated the ability to be reliable. Consistency is a major factor in you completing your earthly assignment.

A Prayer for Consistency

Father, I thank You for showing me what consistency looks like. Reveal the areas in my life where I have not been consistent. Show me where the distractions are, and I will be more intentional about devoting my time and energy to those things that will profit and deliver kingdom results. Amen

Reflection Questions

If you need more space to record your thoughts, feel free to use the chapter journal in the back of this book.

1. In what area can you be more consistent?

2. Share an opportunity that you missed because you failed to be consistent.

3. Review the Components of Kingdom Consistency section. Which principle resonates with you the most? Why?

Chapter 7

The Journey to Completion

"For I am already being poured out like a drink offering, and the time for my departure is near. I have fought the good fight, I have finished the race, I have kept the faith."

2 Timothy 4:6

I read a sign once that said, "If God seems far away, guess who moved?" The more I get to know God's character, I discover more of His rich anticipation for His people. His provision brings the power to choose. We get to choose whether or not we receive it. And more often than not, we make that decision in our hearts first and then with our actions. The journey to completion requires us to stay committed to God's best for us. That commitment is powered by our relationship with Him. It has immediate and eternal implications.

Yes, our choices can impact the livelihood of others. Adam and Eve had a choice to stay plugged in to God's influence, but they chose otherwise. And their eagerness to chase an alternate desire set the stage for the rest of humanity to do the same. God's definitive objective for creation was to forever be in an intimate relationship with us. But because of our flesh, we break that intimacy, and we remain in a constant battle to maintain our legal place of relationship with Him. Not because he took it away, but because we've walked away or have somehow been drawn away. But why do we walk away or allow ourselves to be manipulated out of our position? What is it that leads us down a trail of progressive decline? Could it be that we don't see the value in giving up something good for something great? This sounds too elementary doesn't it? At a fundamental level, it's about value perception. We invest in what we value. It's a simple principle that introduced sin into the world.

Eve valued the opportunity to match God's knowledge, versus resting in God's presence and provision. Adam valued Eve's approval over God's directives. They perceived that the fruit from the tree of the knowledge of good and evil was better than living a lifestyle of intimacy with God, and we've been struggling to get back to that place ever since. Throughout the Bible, we see man electing to substitute God's will for his own; epic stories of people who opted out of a life of favor and grace to pursue their agenda only to discover that God's will is superior to man's genius. One such story is that of a young man who had it all, lost it all, but he was restored because of his father's love. He has been identified as the prodigal son. This popular parable can be found in Luke 15:11-32.

There is a direct correlation between the prodigal son and our relationship with God. Here we have a rich father who loved his sons so much that he made provisions for them to prosper for years to come. Nothing in his house was off-limits to them; all that belonged to the father belonged to them. The young men wanted for nothing. And yet, the youngest son stood before his father with corrupted confidence and asked for his inheritance. But what the young man didn't realize is that he was asking for a smaller portion of all that he had access to. The father obliged, and the stench of the son's pride progressed. In Luke 15:11-13, we see how the son avoided a covenant relationship with his father and settled for convenient associations. Convenient associations are contingent upon you producing and others consuming. When you refuse to accommodate their entitlement, it can have an adverse effect on the relationship. If you recall the story I told you about my friend who wanted to ride in my parents' car but refused to give me gas money, there's a difference between supporters and contributors. Supporters want to ride in the car with you, but contributors will help you reach your goal. Only one is willing to sacrifice a piece of themselves for the mission. Covenant relationships require more of a personal investment, but they help to fuel your destiny.

In Luke 15:15, the son settled in a place beneath his status & accepted conditions that didn't reflect his true value. Have you ever asked yourself, "How did I get here?" If you trace your steps, you will find that your desires began to trump God's desires somewhere along the way. Luke 15:16 finds the son lowering his expectations and standards just to be filled, but he wasn't fulfilled.

I've seen how this has played out in the lives of so many talented and anointed people. They didn't want to be lonely, so they attached themselves to the first person or idea that served their insecurities. They wanted to be accepted so bad that they were willing to live a lie just to be included. They filled an empty space, but they weren't fulfilled. It was just something to do.

A major threat to you completing your assignment is the absence of a consistent relationship with the Father. The relationship is the answer. Clarity of purpose is found there. Direction and strategy abide there. Real love and the advantage of grace are two pillars that hold it together. As you navigate the halls of your assignment, remember to do what's necessary. Take inventory of what you value because that will drive your decisions. Be mindful of how you feel, but don't be led by your feelings. Remain consistent even when you don't feel like it. Get out of your head. Be careful not to substitute God's provision for a strategy that you want to control. Eliminate distractions and remain diligent in your work. The enemy will use every trick in his bag to try to pull you away, but there is too much at stake. Diligence doesn't always look pretty and sometimes it doesn't feel good, but the payout is worth it.

Kingdom confidence is a perpetual rhythm of unlearning, development, and alignment. See it through to the end. And hopefully, someday, when your time on earth has commenced, people will study your life and say that you were committed to ending well.

A Prayer for Completion

Father, amid my accolades and good deeds, You alone are worthy of being acknowledged. I am nothing without You. My confidence resides in You and not my strength. I want You to be glorified in my life. Help me to complete my earthly assignment with grace. May the seed of my assignment give birth to the greater works in someone else's life. Amen.

Reflection Questions

If you need more space to record your thoughts, feel free to use the chapter journal in the back of this book.

1. In what way has your life resembled that of the prodigal son's?

2. Identify the people who have contributed to you demonstrating your assignment. Who are they? What characteristics do they share?

3. In terms of completing your earthly assignment, what habits or behaviors do you need to correct to ensure that your work on earth is not in vain? Why?

CONCLUSION

As you have read, there is a special type of soul work that is required to carry Kingdom Confidence. It's not for the faint at heart because the opposition you will encounter can be treacherous at times. There will be occasions when it seems like you're standing still, and everyone else will appear to be moving at a faster pace and achieving their destiny quicker than you are. You may even feel like you've subscribed to an old fashioned way of achieving success. When you are tempted to abandon your work, remember that Kingdom Confidence is not just another trend to follow; this is our way of life!

As you grow in your Kingdom Confidence, you might receive awkward stares and cynical rebuttals from those who simply don't understand. And that's fine; it's expected even. Don't lash out. Walk in the fruit of the spirit. The results of Kingdom Confidence are not measured by the same standards that your industry follows. This is different, much different. In your moments of doubt, no matter how small or extreme they are, be encouraged that you've committed to building a catalogue of obedience. That track record will push you to complete your assignment the way that God intended.

Unlike Moses, who succumbed to the people's pressure and smote the rock versus speaking to it like God commanded him to, your courage to be obedient will give you access to more than you could ever work for. Obedience is a relationship builder. I mentioned it earlier, and I'll share it again here, the relationship gives us access to knowledge and resources that we didn't have to work, hustle, and grind for.

So, when you feel the need to throw away the confidence that you've invested in, you don't have to be ashamed about how you feel, but you can find comfort in knowing that you can approach God with boldness because He has given you everything you need for life and godliness. He is the source of your kingdom's confidence.

ABOUT THE AUTHOR

Jesse Cole is the COO (Chief Obedience Officer) of Kingdom Mogul Coaching. A coaching and consulting company that helps business leaders grow their faith as they grow their business. As an author, professional speaker, coach, husband and father, Jesse believes that his purpose in life is to encourage and equip leaders to become the better version of themselves.

Jesse's relatable presence appeals to those who believe that there is no separation between their real life and the service they provide. Using his framework of "Graceful Accountability" he helps his clients build and monetize their kingdom platforms using their God-given talents while showing up in the marketplace with authenticity and boldness.

Learn More About Jesse
www.Facebook.com/CoachJesseCole
www.Instagram.com/CoachJesseCole
www.CoachJesseCole.com

Notes From Chapter 1

Notes From Chapter 2

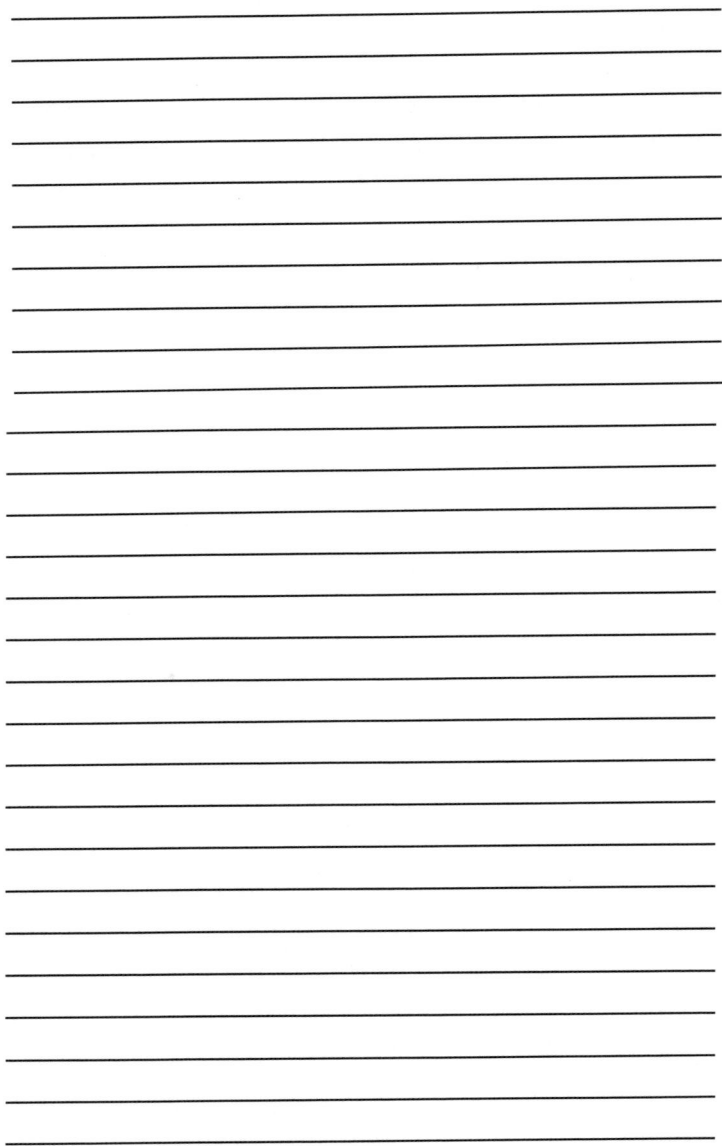

Notes From Chapter 3

Notes From Chapter 4

Notes From Chapter 5

Notes From Chapter 6

_____
_____
_____
_____
_____
_____
_____
_____
_____
_____
_____
_____
_____
_____
_____
_____
_____
_____
_____
_____
_____

Notes From Chapter 7

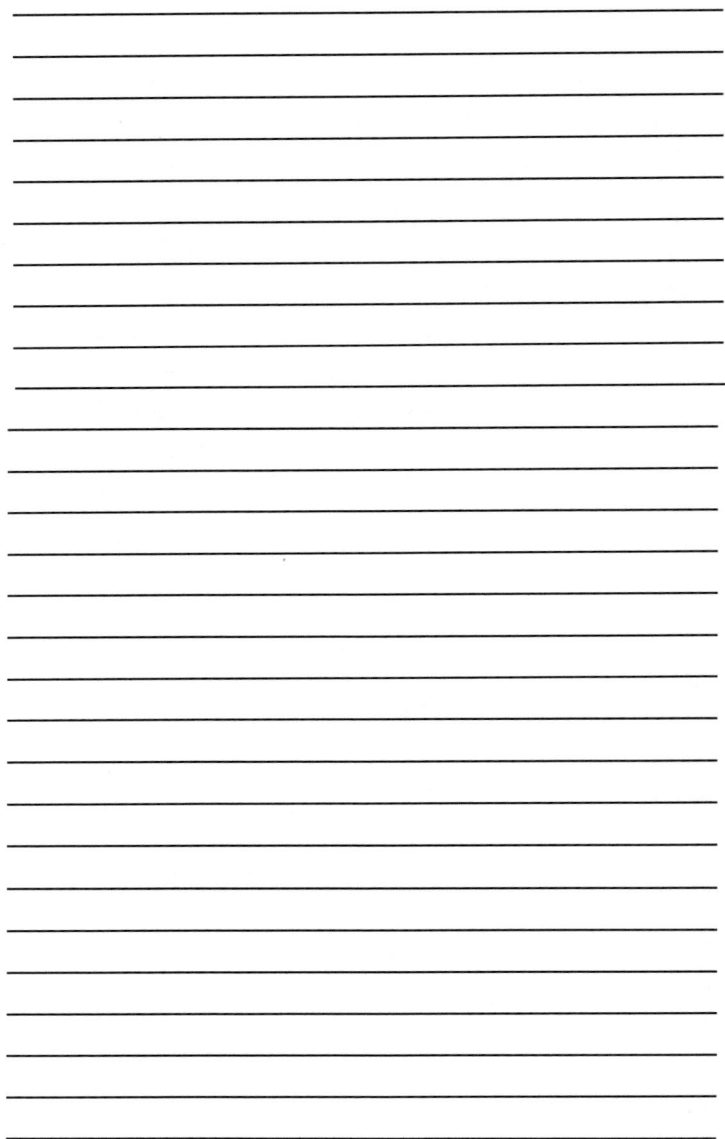

Made in the USA
Middletown, DE
28 September 2022